Be Kind to Your Mother (Earth) and Blame It on the Wolf

Two Original Plays

Be Kind to Your Mother (Earth) and Blame It on the Wolf

Two Original Plays

by Douglas Love

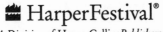 HarperFestival®
A *Division of* HarperCollins*Publishers*

Library of Congress Cataloging-in-Publication Data
Love, Douglas.
  [Be kind to your Mother (Earth)]
  Be kind to your Mother (Earth) ; and Blame it on the wolf : two original plays / by Douglas Love.
      p.   cm.
  Summary: Two plays, one featuring time-traveling environmentalists concerned about saving the Earth and the other highlighting characters from traditional fairy tales telling alternative versions of their stories.
  ISBN 0-06-021106-7 (lib. bdg.)
  1. Children's plays, American.   [1. Plays.]   I. Love, Douglas. Blame it on the wolf.   1992.   II. Title.
PS3562.O839B4   1992
812'.54—dc20
                                              92-4624
                                                CIP
                                                 AC

For my family: Beverly, Martin, Darcy, and Lauren

CONTENTS

Introduction

Welcome to the exciting, fantastic, inspiring, and always surprising world of the theatre. The written script that the playwright provides is only the beginning. A script is meant to be used like a map. It is the route that will guide you through the story. The adventures that you have while rehearsing and performing the play are up to you. Every part of putting on a play can be a different adventure. Costumes, props, and sets can be fun and exciting projects that involve everyone.

Because the actors are right in front of an audience—live (not up on a movie screen or inside a television)—anything can happen, and it usually does. Scenery may fall over, people may say the wrong lines at the wrong time or forget their lines altogether. When these mistakes happen, the actors can't stop and start over. In the theatre, they go right on and try to get back on track with as much ease as possible. That is the challenge of live theatre. The feeling that *anything can happen* keeps the actors on their toes.

While working on the production, don't be discouraged if you feel that you don't have the exact prop or costume that the play calls for. If the stage directions ask for a couch in a certain scene, there is no rule that says you can't use a bench, or a chair, or nothing at all instead. You read through the play and decide what you think is important to include and what you are able to include. If you are playing an astronaut on the moon and the stage directions tell you to take off your space helmet, don't worry if you don't have a space helmet; use a bicycle helmet or a baseball cap, or just pretend to take off the helmet! Some of the best plays have no props or stage settings at all. The audience is able to use its imagination. That can be fun for the audience! They can feel that they have a special part in making the play. People's imaginations draw them into the performance as an active participant.

It is almost always helpful to have someone serve as the director of the play, whether you are performing in your school or your backyard. This person will help make decisions about the direction your production takes: Will everyone wear costumes? Will you make a set? Who will play which character? He or she may also designate certain parts of the stage to be different places where the action takes place. The director should also help everyone working on the play realize that the theatre is a collaborative art. This means that the talents of a lot of people come together to create one exciting production that everyone can be proud of because everyone helped to create it.

Performers have a special task in the play. Once a director has assigned roles, the next step is to develop a character. This is achieved by asking yourself a lot of questions: If I was this person (or animal), how would I walk? How would I stand? How would I speak? What would I wear? Whom do I like in the play? Whom don't I like in the play? What do I want to do in the play? You can and should ask yourself these and more questions about your character. Then, you have to answer these questions and make some decisions. If you are playing an old man, you might decide to stand hunched over and walk with a cane. You may choose to have a gravelly voice and tattered clothes. You may discover while reading the play that you are a rich old man who doesn't spend any of his money, and you are afraid that everyone is trying to steal it.

The answers and decisions that you make about your character are guideposts on your journey through your production. It's okay to change your mind if something is not working. None of the choices that you make for your character are wrong. Some choices work better than others. Experiment! That's what rehearsals are for.

If you plan to perform this play for an audience, I would like to impress upon you the importance of rehearsal. Some theatre directors and actors believe that you should rehearse one hour for every minute that you are on stage. Some of that rehearsal time can be spent on your own, memorizing your lines. Different people memorize lines differently, but all techniques have one thing in common—repetition. Go over and over and over your lines until you can say them without looking at the script. Some people sit alone reading their lines again and again until they can say them from memory. Others read their lines into a tape recorder and listen to the tape over and over. Or ask a friend or someone in your family to "hold book." This means that they read the line that comes before yours and then you say your line.

Rehearsal is also the time to decide on your blocking, or the physical action of the play. Who does what, when? If everything is planned before the performance, you'll feel more secure, and the audience will be able to follow the story more easily.

When planning your blocking, remember that you are performing for an audience that needs to see what is going on to follow the story of the play. Important action should take place closer to the audience. Try to face the audience as much as possible; this allows them to see your facial expressions and hear you better.

Each of these plays has many characters. If you are working with a smaller group, it is easy for the same actor to play many parts in the same performance. You can change characters by changing a hat or your voice or the way that you walk. There are two cast lists for each play to help you with this "doubling."

Whether you will be performing on your school stage, in your classroom, or at your home, I wrote this play for you to read and enjoy. Feel free to make changes to make the play work for you, and use it as a jumping off point into the unlimited world of your own creativity and imagination.

Be Kind to Your Mother (Earth)

Characters

In the year 2053:
  Grandma Jones
  Grandchild Jones

In the year 1993:
  Chester
  DeeDee
  Kato
  Papa Picnic
  Patty Picnic
  PeeWee Picnic
  Mother Nature
  The Children of the Atmosphere
    (minimum of 3 actors)
  Benny, the used time machine salesman
  Grandpa Garbage, the villain!

The Boston Tea Party, 1773:
  The colonists: Marnie, Tom, Jean, Pete, Sam,
    Jessica

At Mount Vernon, 1738:
  George Washington
    (as a boy with a cherry tree)
  George's mom

Dodo Island, 1500's:
  The Dodo Birdies: Dotty, Dingy, Dizzy, Daffy, Mama
    Dodo, Baby Dodo

6

Optional Casting—11 actors

Chester

DeeDee

Kato

Grandpa Garbage

Actor 1—Grandma Jones, Marnie, Dotty

Actor 2—Grandchild Jones, Child of the
Atmosphere, Dingy, Jessica

Actor 3—Papa Picnic, Tom, George Washington,
Dizzy

Actor 4—Patty Picnic, Child of the Atmosphere,
Jean, Mama Dodo

Actor 5—PeeWee Picnic, Child of the Atmosphere,
Pete

Actor 6—Mother Nature, George's Mom, Daffy

Actor 7—Benny, Sam, Baby Dodo

★ *The above is only a suggestion and can be done
with even fewer actors by cutting some of the
Dodos and colonists.*

★ *For more parts you can add more Children of
the Atmosphere.*

Scene 1

★ GRANDMA JONES *is getting* GRANDCHILD JONES *ready for bed. There is one single bed stage left. Just right of the bed is a rocking chair. There is a window upstage right that can open and close.*

Grandchild: Grandma, I don't want to go to bed yet. I'm not tired! Let me stay up and demoleculize something.

Grandma: You're not tired? You've been running around here all day! Not only that, we went to the planetarium and the jet propulsion center and we toured the meteorite! I'm worn out!

Grandchild: I'm not! I want to hear a story!

Grandma: A story! Goldilocks and the Three Androids? Or Little Red Shooting Star?

Grandchild: That's kid's stuff! I want to hear a real story!

★ *At that moment, debris flies in the window. It is pollution.*

Grandma: Oh, dear! *(She crosses to shut the window.)* The pollution level is so high today!

8

Grandchild: They finally plowed a path through the old park. Before that we couldn't even walk through it, there was so much garbage! It smelled really bad too! P.U.! Were things this polluted when you were a kid, Grandma?

Grandma: There was pollution. That's for sure. But not this bad. We used to be able to look out the window of a four-story building and see the ground when we looked down. Now all you see is smog, and if you could see the ground, you'd see that it's covered with garbage.

Grandchild: Why does the sun shine only twelve minutes a day?

Grandma: That's air pollution, dear. It's caused a haze all around the planet.

Grandchild: Yuck.

Grandma: Yuck is right. If we didn't have air purifying systems in our homes, we'd never breathe clean air. *(Thinking it over)* You want to hear a story? I've got a story for you. It's a true story too! When I was your age, back in 1993 . . .

Grandchild: 1993! Wow, you're old! Did they have dinosaurs back then?

Grandma: No, dear. Listen to Grandma's story. Back in 1993, I knew three kids who were very upset about the condition of the environment.

Grandchild: So there *was* pollution back in the dark ages.

★ *Lights dim.*

★ *The stage changes to represent a change in time. This can be achieved by the actors moving offstage in slow motion and the next group of actors moving onstage in slow motion. (There could also be signs that are flipped with the years printed on them. These signs could remain onstage and change each time the action of the play moves into another year.)*

★ *End of Scene*

Scene 2

★ *Three kids,* CHESTER, DEEDEE, *and* KATO, *sit near a pond, relaxing. A group of kids on a picnic with* GRANDPA GARBAGE *and his son,* PAPA, *run onstage and start to pollute the entire area.*

Grandpa Garbage: Come on! Come on over here! I found a great spot for us to picnic!

Papa: Come on, kids! Patty! PeeWee! This way! Grandpa's found us a spot. *(He begins to stretch out a picnic blanket.)*

Patty: I don't like this spot! Yuck! You're not going to lay that blanket on the yuckie ground! In the dirt!

Papa: Ah! A little dirt never hurt anybody! Besides, I'm hungry! I didn't want to go on this picnic! It was all your grandpa's idea.

Grandpa Garbage: Come on, kids! We have some good food here! Here *(handing some sandwiches to* PEEWEE*),* pass these out.

PeeWee: Goodie, goodie, goodie!

Patty: What should I do with the wrapper?

Papa: Just throw it in the water. It doesn't matter. Just look around. There's so much pollution, a few more wrappers aren't going to make any difference.

★ *They proceed to eat things and throw their garbage all over the stage.*

Patty: I'm done!

Papa: I'm done!

PeeWee: I'm done!

Grandpa Garbage: You all run along and play. I'll catch up to you.

★ *PAPA, PATTY, and PEEWEE exit. GRANDPA GARBAGE hides in the corner and listens to CHESTER, DEEDEE, and KATO's conversation.*

Chester: Did you see that? They just threw all of their garbage all over the place.

Kato: Some of it went into our pond!

DeeDee: Wait a minute! I think I've got something!

Kato: Pull it in!

★ *DEEDEE has been fishing in the pond all this time. She reels in her catch. It is an old shoe.*

Chester: That's it! I'm going to complain to someone!

Kato: To whom?

Chester: I don't know! To our congressperson!

Kato: We're just kids! They're not going to listen to us. We have to find someone with power! With experience! With the ability to get the job done!

DeeDee *(looking offstage)*: Someone's coming!

★ *MOTHER NATURE enters with THE CHILDREN OF THE ATMOSPHERE.*

Mother Nature: Children! Try to stay in line! Don't get lost! Here, here. Let's stop and rest a moment! Dip your tiny toes in the pond.

DeeDee: Who are you?

Mother Nature: Who are you!?

DeeDee: I asked you first.

Mother Nature: What does that have to do with the price of potatoes?

DeeDee: The price of what?

Mother Nature: Potatoes!

DeeDee: I don't know. What DOES it have to do with the price of potatoes?

Mother Nature: I asked you first.

DeeDee: I'm so confused!

Mother Nature: I was just fooling, dear! That was just an expression.

DeeDee: Oh, well, then I was just fooling too.

★ *There is a clap of thunder and some lightning.*

Mother Nature: It's not nice to fool Mother Nature!

DeeDee: I'm still confused!

Chester: You're Mother Nature? Wow! Am I glad that you came along. We need to talk! There is far too much littering and polluting going on around here!

Kato: Just look around! There is garbage everywhere! And this is from only one family!

Mother Nature: You don't have to tell me about pollution. Pollution has been around for centuries! I do fear that it will stick around for centuries more.

Chester: If it sticks around there won't be more centuries. Soon all the garbage will take over, and we'll all be in it up to our eyebrows!

Mother Nature: You can't change the past! People are used to littering! They don't understand that when they throw their trash on the ground or in the water, it hurts our environment. And they're cutting down trees, not to mention the number of endangered species there are now.

DeeDee: What can we do?

Mother Nature: I wish I knew. The condition of the earth is making my Children of the Atmosphere quite ill. Every time someone throws garbage on the ground, or out their car window or into our rivers, lakes, and oceans, my Children of the Atmosphere get very, very sick. (*THE CHILDREN OF THE ATMOSPHERE cough and moan.*)

Mother Nature: Well, we must be running along. This so-called fresh air isn't good for my children.

★ *They exit.*

Kato: I don't get it. Why did people start littering and cutting down trees?

Chester: You heard what Mother Nature said. They're used to it. They've been doing it for centuries.

Kato: If only we could go back and tell them not to start!

DeeDee: We'd need some kind of time machine to do that.

★ *Used time machine salesman* BENNY *enters with a* boing!

Benny: Did someone say that they needed a time machine?

DeeDee: Who are you?

Benny: Benny! I sell time machines—new and used. I've also got watches. *(BENNY rolls up his jacket sleeve to show watches strapped all the way up his arm.)*

Kato: We need a time machine!

Benny: You're in luck. I got my last one—still available.

Chester: New or used?

Benny: Used—but only by a little old lady who used to take it to the seventeenth century on Sundays.

Kato: How much?

★ BENNY *whispers a figure into* KATO's *ear.* KATO *whispers into* CHESTER's *ear.* CHESTER *whispers into* DEEDEE's *ear.*

DeeDee: What?!

Chester and **Kato** *(covering her mouth)*: Shh!

Chester *(to BENNY)*: We have to talk it over. *(They huddle.)*

Kato: We can't afford that! All I've got on me is 37 cents.

Chester: I only have $2.53 at home, and I was saving it for a rainy day.

DeeDee: Don't look at me! I don't have any money.

Chester: We only need it for one day! *(He gets a bright idea and turns to BENNY.)* We thought it over, and we would like it, but we'd have to take it for a test drive first.

Benny: Well . . .

DeeDee: I thought we only needed it for one . . . *(KATO stops her before she spills the beans.)*

Benny: What . . . ?

Kato: Umm. . . . We only need one test drive and then we'll decide!

Chester: We'll be back soon.

Kato: Just once around the millennium, you know.

Benny: All right. Don't be long! *(He exits.)*

★ *The kids go over to the machine.*

DeeDee: Wow! A real time machine.

Kato: What do we do now?

DeeDee: Simple! Don't you see? If we can go back in time and convince people to stop littering and cutting down trees, then their children won't . . . and their children won't . . . and their children won't . . . and their children won't either.

Chester: That's a great idea, DeeDee!

DeeDee: It is?

Kato: Sure! But we don't have much time. We'll have to visit very famous people—so the whole world can learn from their example.

DeeDee: Where should we go first?

Chester: Let's do something to clean up the harbors, rivers, oceans, and ponds!

Kato: Let's see. Who were the first people to pollute the water?

Chester: I've got it!

★ *The three of them pop into the time machine and it takes off.*

★ GRANDPA GARBAGE *emerges from the corner where he has been hiding all along.*

Grandpa Garbage: So, they think that they can clean up the past, do they? They want to get rid of all my beautiful garbage, do they? They think they're the only ones who can get a time machine, do they? Well, do they?

★ BENNY *enters.*

Benny: Did someone say that they needed a time machine?

Grandpa Garbage: What?

Benny: Benny's the name. I sell time machines— new and used. I also got watches. *(BENNY rolls up his jacket sleeve to show his watches.)*

Grandpa Garbage: I need a time machine!

Benny: You're in luck. I got my last one—still available. Step this way. I'll show it to ya!

★ *They exit.*

★ *End of Scene*

Scene 3

The Boston Tea Party

★ *Time: Year 1773*

★ *The stage is set to look like a dock as if the water is beyond the downstage edge where the audience is sitting. A rope can be set up across the front of the stage about three feet high to show the edge of the dock. Fishing nets and coiled rope can be used to decorate the upstage areas. There are three large crates downstage right that have the word "TEA" painted on the side. The colonists* JEAN, TOM, *and* MARNIE *enter, in traditional Native American dress.*

Jean: This new land promises great freedoms for all colonists.

Tom: I see great happiness here. We shall overcome the oppression of the King!

★ PETE *runs on. He is dressed in traditional Native American dress. He has a headband without a feather.*

Pete: We are almost ready for you. Do you have the feathers?

Jean: Yes, here they are. *(She hands him some feathers.)*

Tom: Is all of the tea loaded on the boat?

Pete: Oh, yes! The boat is full of tea!

★ SAM *and* JESSICA *enter.*

Sam: Pete, we are ready!

Jessica: Those redcoats will be surprised when we toss their tea in the harbor!

Pete: We will show them that our freedom will not be threatened by taxes on tea.

Sam: We will gladly go without tea for a year rather than pay their tax!

Jessica: We will go without tea for ten years!

Marnie: I will gladly give up tea for fifteen years.

Jean: I like tea. I have six cups a day—very hot with cream and sugar. I especially like it in the morning with a biscuit and orange marmalade.

Jessica: Don't you want to put an end to the oppression of the King?

Pete: We have to make a statement!

Jean: Couldn't we just send him a letter?

Marnie *(pointing offstage)*: Look!

Tom: Where?

Jean: Look at that house that has fallen from the sky . . . next to the ship.

Tom: Is it a demon?

Marnie: Or a spirit?

★ *CHESTER, DEEDEE, and KATO enter.*

Chester: Hello!

DeeDee and **Kato:** Hi!

Pete: Who are you?

Chester: My name is Chester.

Sam: Are you a demon?

Jessica: Or a spirit?

Chester: I'm just a kid.

Jean: What about your friends? Are they spirits?

Kato: No! We've come to convince you not to spill the tea into the harbor.

Marnie: They must be redcoats!

Tom: But how would the redcoats know that we were going to spill the tea?

Jean: Spies!

DeeDee: No! We are Americans!

Pete: You don't look like anyone I know.

Kato: That's not important. We don't have much time.

Chester: You can't put all that tea in the water. You'll pollute it!

Jessica: But we have to make a statement.

Pete: We are being taxed unfairly.

Kato: Boycott the tax. Refuse to pay it! If you dump all that tea into the water, where will it go? Who will clean it up? Think of the fish.

DeeDee: The fish might not even be thirsty!

Kato: What if everyone just went around dumping things into the water?

Chester: Think how dirty it would become.

Tom: I like to swim in the water. I wouldn't like to swim in a place full of garbage.

Marnie: I wash my clothes with the same water. I would not like to wash clothes with dirty water.

Jean: And I like tea! Why waste it? If you are spirits we thank you for your guidance.

Chester: We're glad to help. Come on.

★ *He exits with the other kids.*

Jean: Well, now what should we do?

Tom: Let's go over to my house. Maybe we'll see Paul Revere.

Jean: Did you hear his latest? Last night he opened his window and yelled, "The British are humming! The British are humming!"

Tom: Humming? What were they humming?

Jean: "God Save the King" no doubt!

★ *They all laugh and exit.*

★ *GRANDPA GARBAGE sneaks on and dumps the tea into the harbor, himself.*

Grandpa Garbage: Little cleanies!

★ *End of Scene*

Scene 4

George Washington's Hill

★ *Time: Year 1738*

★ GEORGE *and his* MOM *enter.*

Mom: Now, George, you pick all the ripe cherries from the tree.

George: All of them?

Mom: Oh, yes. I promised some to Aunt Louise and Uncle Sebastian. I should also send some over to Noonie and Ah-hah.

George: Noonie and Ah-hah? They have their own cherry tree! And Noonie always pinches my cheeks and always calls me Georgie-Porgie. Why can't they eat their own cherries?

Mom: Well, they're getting old, dear. They don't have a big strong son to reach the high ones. Oh, I almost forgot the Jeffersons. Better pick another peck for them. Proceed to pick your pecks, George.

★ *She exits.*

George (*Imitating his mother in a voice too soft for her to hear*): Proceed to pick your pecks, George.

★ *CHESTER, DEEDEE, and KATO enter.*

Chester *(pointing at GEORGE)*: There he is! Let's wait back here and see what happens.

DeeDee: That's the father of our country? He looks a little young.

Chester: This is when he was still a boy. He cut down a cherry tree.

DeeDee: Why?

Kato: I don't know—but we'd better find out if we want to stop him.

George *(talking to himself)*: Every year it's the same thing. Pick the cherries, pick the cherries, all day, every day. I wish I didn't have this stupid tree. *(George swings his ax and is about to chop down the tree.)*

DeeDee *(crossing down to GEORGE)*: That's not very nice. Trees are important.

George: Who are you?

DeeDee: I am a friend of all trees.

George: Well, this tree is not my friend. Every year it grows cherries, and every year I have to pick them. I'd much rather be playing. I don't even like cherries.

DeeDee: This tree is helping you breathe.

George: It is? How?

DeeDee: Trees give us oxygen.

George: Who cares about oxygen?

★ *KATO comes down to meet them.*

Kato: Who cares about oxygen?

George: Who are you?

Kato: A friend of oxygen.

George: Who needs oxygen?

Kato: We all need oxygen to live!

DeeDee: Animals need oxygen too! Dogs, cats, cows, goats, horses . . .

George: Even duckies?

★ *DEEDEE, CHESTER, and KATO look at each other.*

DeeDee: Especially duckies!

Chester: The air is getting more and more polluted. We need trees to clean up the air!

George *(still thinking about the duckies)*: Even

duckies need oxygen? I wouldn't like
to cut down the tree if it would mean less oxygen
for duckies. I will not cut it down.
I will pick the pecks that mother asked for. With
each peck I shall think of the little duckies that are
breathing the oxygen from my tree.

Kato: That's great. We have to go now. We're
running out of time!

DeeDee: It was nice meeting you, Mr. President.

George: Oh no, my last name is Washington.

DeeDee: Oh, sorry. 'Bye.

★ *They exit.*

George: I'd better go around back and get the cherry
baskets.

★ *He exits. GRANDPA GARBAGE enters and chops
down the cherry tree. He cackles in delight and
exits.*

★ *End of Scene*

Scene 5

Dodo Island

★ *Time: 1500's*

★ *There are three trees placed across center stage—one left, one right, and one exactly center. The center tree is the one that the Dodos will circle later in the scene. The tree should be colorful and taller than the tallest actor in the play. The temperature on the island is very hot. Actors should imagine that the ground is covered with sand.*

★ CHESTER, KATO, DEEDEE *enter the stage from the time machine.*

DeeDee: Where are we?

Kato: I don't know. I just punched in "extinct animals" and this is where we ended up.

Chester: I wonder what year we're in.

DeeDee: Someone's coming.

Chester: Let's wait back here out of sight.

★ *The three of them hide near the back of the stage.*

★ DOTTY, *a Dodo bird, comes out.*

Dotty: Food. *Wok!* Food. *Wok! Wok!* (*She continues to search for food. She occasionally bumps into objects.*)

Chester: Could it be? I think it is . . .

Kato: Is what? Is what?

Chester: That, my friends, is an Apoxicus Dobirdacus.

DeeDee: Acopa what? Daberda who?

Chester: A Dodo bird.

DeeDee: Let's go talk to it.

Chester: No, we might scare it. Let's watch a little longer.

★ DIZZY *enters looking worried.*

Dizzy: Did you find him?

Dotty: No. *Wok!* I've been looking behind this tree for hours.

Dizzy: You looked for him behind this tree?

Dotty: I cannot get behind it.

Dizzy: And why not?

Dotty: I have spent a long time looking behind this tree for him. Yet, every time I go behind the tree, I look and there is suddenly another side to go behind. Just watch. Let's look for him behind this tree. *(They both walk around the tree.)* Now look! There is still another side to go behind.

Dizzy: Then let us go behind it. *(They walk back to the downstage side of the tree.)* I see your dilemma.

★ *DINGY enters.*

Dingy: There you both are. Have you found him?

Dotty: No. We are trying to look behind this tree, yet it is quite impossible.

Dizzy: What if he is behind the tree and we never know?

Dingy: Oh, our poor baby brother.

★ *DAFFY enters. DIZZY crosses to him.*

Dizzy: Have you found our baby brother yet?

Daffy: We're still searching for him. Have you?

Dizzy: Mama will not be happy if we can't find Baby.

Daffy: She will scold us for sure.

Dizzy: We must not dawdle. We must discover some way to get behind this tree.

★ *CHESTER, DEEDEE, and KATO are watching this scene.*

Chester *(to DEEDEE)***:** The Dodo birds are extinct now.

DeeDee *(to CHESTER)***:** What does extinct mean?

Chester: It means that they aren't anymore. There are none left.

DeeDee: Where are they?

Kato: They didn't survive.

DeeDee: Is that what people mean when they talk about endangered species?

Chester: Those are animals that are in danger of not surviving. They can't adapt to the changing environment.

DeeDee: They're not smart enough to adapt?

Kato: In some places in 1993, DeeDee, man is destroying the environment so fast that the animals have no place to live or get food.

DeeDee: That's terrible. How can we help?

Chester: Well, maybe if we take a Dodo bird back with us to 1993, it can tell us what's different about the way we live in the future.

DeeDee: Let's do it. We'd be the only kids with a pet Dodo!

Kato: Which Dodo should we bring back with us?

Chester: Maybe we should look for this baby Dodo. Then we could teach it all about the future—and it could lead a happy, long life!

Kato: Well, let's look around!

★ *The three of them exit.*

★ *MAMA DODO comes on searching.*

Mama: My poor baby. I miss him so. A child so young needs his mother to help and keep him, to teach him the way. Like my dear mother taught me and her dear mother taught her and her mother taught her and her mother taught her and her mother . . . . *(to audience)* Can you see the pattern here? You see . . .

A Dodo's a bird like no other;
It should not be apart from its mother.
It will sniffle so sadly
And feel, well, quite badly.
And its wings do not fly, soar or hover.

My poor baby! *(Runs off crying.)*

★ *BABY wanders in.*

Baby: If I walk 72 steps this way and 49 steps that way, I am sure to be back at the nest.

★ *CHESTER, DEEDEE, and KATO walk in.*

Chester: Look—there it is! The baby Dodo bird!

DeeDee: Grab him!

Kato: No, DeeDee. We have to talk to him. Tell him about our plan.

DeeDee: Then grab him?

Chester: No, DeeDee! We have to convince him that it is a good idea for him to come with us to 1993.

DeeDee: How are we going to do that? We only have a few more minutes left before we have to return the time machine to Benny!

Kato: What are we wasting time for? Let's go talk to the bird! *(She crosses to BABY.)* Hi, I'm Kato.

Baby: I'm lost. I'm looking for the rest of my family. Are you lost too?

Chester: No. Why do you ask?

Baby: I've never seen you around here before.

Kato: We're not from around here. We're from the future.

Baby: Is that farther than the farthest mountain?

DeeDee: Oh, yes. We're from another time!

Chester: We've come to bring you back with us.

Kato: We are from the year 1993.

Baby: That is far away. What happens in 1993? Are there many successful Dodos there?

Chester: Not exactly.

DeeDee: Actually, the Dodo has become extinct at the time we are from. There are no more of you.

Chester: That is why we want you to come back with us and give the Dodo a future.

Baby: Would I be very popular?

Chester: Oh, yes! When people hear that there is a real Dodo in 1993, they will certainly stop and take notice.

Baby: Then I will go with you. I have many sisters, and I often get lost in the shuffle. That is how I became lost today.

Chester: Come on, guys. Let's bring the baby Dodo back to 1993 with us and see what effects our Boston Tea Party and George Washington work has had.

★ *They exit with* BABY.

★ *End of Scene*

Scene 6

The Pond

★ *Time: Year 1993*

★ *The pond is still in the same mess that the kids left it in. The work that they did in the time machine did nothing to help the environment.*

Kato *(running on):* Here we are, back at the great, big, beautiful . . . *(looking around)* polluted, dirty, garbage pond!

Chester: I don't understand it. I thought that we could make a difference! All of our hard work and traveling was for nothing!

DeeDee: I don't get it. Why didn't it help? I thought that we were coming back to a brand new and improved 1993. Instead, it is just as dirty and polluted as we left it.

Chester: So much for time travel chain reactions.

Kato: I can't believe that we did all that for nothing.

★ *They all sit in despair amidst the pollution.*

DeeDee: Well, at least we have a pet Dodo bird!

37

Baby *(sneezing)*: *A-choo! A-choo!* I can't stop . . . *A-choo!* sneezing! *A-choo!*

Kato: What's the matter with him?

Baby: *A-choo!* This isn't as fun as I thought, *A-choo!*, it would be! *A-choo!*

Chester: Maybe he's allergic to the air. After all, nothing we did in the time machine did anything to make the land, water, or air any cleaner!

Baby: *A-choo!* I want my, *A-choo!*, mommy! *(BABY starts to cry and sneeze at the same time.)*

DeeDee: What are we going to do now? Baby wants his mommy!

Chester: We better send him back home. I can set the controls on the time machine to bring Baby back to his nest and then return itself to Benny. *(to BABY)* Come on, Baby. You're going home.

★ *CHESTER and BABY exit.*

★ *GRANDMA and GRANDCHILD enter in their own time machine.*

Grandchild: Look, Grandma. There they are!

Kato: Who are you?

Grandma: We're from the future. We came to help.

Chester *(entering)*: Well, Baby's on his way back home. *(to* GRANDMA *and* GRANDCHILD*)* Who are you?

Grandchild: We know about all of your travels.

Grandma: We just wanted to tell you that you are wasting your time.

Chester: We know!

DeeDee: We tried to go back and change things but it didn't work.

Kato: I guess that some things never change.

Grandma: Well, some things DO!

DeeDee: What do you mean?

Grandma: You are concentrating on changing the wrong thing. You have to do something in your own time.

Grandchild: Don't try to change things in somebody else's time!

Grandma: The future is yours. You must make of it what you will. Act today to clean the world for tomorrow.

Chester: I get it! We can only make changes today for tomorrow!

Kato: Don't change yesterday for today!

Chester: What is past is past! We can't fix it.

Kato: We are in charge of what happens today!

DeeDee: I don't get it!

Grandchild: We have to pick up trash and recycle and save trees and animals today so we can enjoy them tomorrow and the day after and the day after and all the days after that.

DeeDee: Wow! You're so smart! It sometimes takes me a while to catch on to things. I guess that will never change.

Chester: Hey, everybody, let's clean up!

★ *GRANDPA GARBAGE enters.*

Grandpa Garbage: No! Don't clean up! Don't clean up my beautiful garbage! If you clean up the earth, you'll destroy me!

★ *No one listens to him and they continue to clean.*

Kato: Hey, this place is looking better already.

Chester: There's just one big piece of garbage to get rid of.

★ *DEEDEE wheels on a big garbage can with a phony lid made of paper so the actor can later break through it.*

DeeDee: Ready!

★ *CHESTER, DEEDEE, and KATO help GRANDPA GARBAGE into the trash can.*

Grandpa Garbage: No! Not my beautiful garbage! Not the can! Anything but the can!

★ *The kids put on the lid.*

Chester, DeeDee, Kato: Done!

★ *At that moment the actor playing GRANDPA GARBAGE breaks through the top of the trash can. He has taken off his outer coat of garbage and is dressed like a regular kid.*

Kato: Who are you?

Grandpa Garbage: Well, I used to be Grandpa Garbage, but, before that, I was just a kid. I remember my mom telling me that if I didn't clean up after myself and stop littering I'd become a "Grandpa Garbage." I didn't know what she meant. I thought everybody littered. Then, one day I woke up

41

and there was garbage all over my room. I did
become a Grandpa Garbage! I don't know how it
happened, maybe it has something to do with the
time travel, but I'm young again! I've got another
chance, and I'll never pollute again!

★ *They all cheer!*

★ *GRANDMA and GRANDCHILD come downstage
away from the group.*

Grandchild: Where are *you,* Grandma?

Grandma: What do you mean?

Grandchild: You said that you knew these kids in
1993. Here we are in 1993. Where are you? We want
to see what you looked like when you were a kid.
(realizing) Your first name is Deirdre, isn't it?

Grandma: Oh, yes. But when I was young, they
used to call me DeeDee.

Grandchild: Wow! Things can change, Grandma!
Things can change!

★ *Curtain*

Blame It on the Wolf

Characters

Wolf
Judge

Jury:
> Tom*
> Sue*
> Ted*
> Ann*
> Pat*
> Sam*

Officer One*
Officer Two*
Officer Three*

The Three Little Pigs:
> Iggie the Piggie*
> Squiggy the Piggie*
> Moe the Piggie*

Hansel*
Gretel*
Woodsman*
Woodswoman*
Witchie Pot Pie
Chicken Little*
Henny Penny*
Turkey Lurkey*
Little Red Riding Hood
Big Red (Little Red's mother)*
Old Red (Little Red's grandmother)*

These parts may be double or triple cast

Optional smaller cast
Actor 1: Wolf
Actor 2: Judge, Big Red
Actor 3: Squiggy the Piggie, Hansel
Actor 4: Iggie the Piggie, Witchie Pot Pie
Actor 5: Moe the Piggie, Gretel, Little Red
Actor 6: Officer One, Chicken Little
Actor 7: Officer Two, Old Red
Actor 8: Officer Three, Turkey Lurkey, Woodsman
Actor 9: Jury (all lines), Woodswoman,
        Henny Penny

★ *This optional smaller cast is only a suggestion.*
You can adapt the cast list for the number of
actors in your group. When using a smaller cast,
keep in mind that you may have to switch lines
around and create early exits to accommodate
quick costume changes. Be creative!

Setting

Upstage center there is a courtroom. Center stage there is a podium for the JUDGE and a chair stage right of the podium for the witness. There are six chairs stage left of the podium for the JURY. Downstage left and right are areas that can be used to create other settings in the play. Tables and chairs can be moved on and set up downstage left to create IGGIE THE PIGGIE's house used in Scenes 2 and 4. Downstage right you can create the outside of WITCHIE POT PIE's candy house used in Scene 6. Downstage left you can set up OLD RED's house in Scene 8 to be used when the Piggie house scenes are over. OLD RED should have a bed with red blankets. During the entire play the courtroom remains onstage. The JUDGE could sit onstage and watch the whole story.

Scene 1: Courtroom
Scene 2: IGGIE THE PIGGIE's brick house
Scene 3: Courtroom
Scene 4: IGGIE THE PIGGIE's brick house
Scene 5: Courtroom
Scene 6: Outside WITCHIE POT PIE's candy house
Scene 7: Courtroom
Scene 8: OLD RED's house
Scene 9: Courtroom

Scene 1

★ *The* JURY *is seated on the stage. The* JUDGE *walks in and steps up to his podium.* WOLF *is downstage center.*

Judge: Jury, have you reached a verdict?

★ *Each jury member stands as they speak.*

Tom: Yes—

Sue: your . . .

Ted: Honor.

Ann: We . . .

Pat: find . . .

Sam: the . . .

Tom: wolf . . .

Wolf: Stop! Wait! Freeze!

★ *All the actors onstage (except* WOLF*) magically freeze, and* WOLF *talks directly to the audience.*

Wolf: I didn't do it! I'm not guilty. You gotta believe me. Why do they always blame the wolf? They never bother to listen to my side of the story—until now! I'm going to tell you my side of the story. You can step into my shoes. You can look through my eyes. You'll decide if I'm guilty. They say that I ate Little Red Riding Hood's grandma, Old Red. I'll present my case, and you can decide. I know you'll be fair. It all started in this courtroom a few days ago when they asked one of the three little pigs to tell the court all about the first time they met me.

★ *The actors move in slow motion to show the change in time, taking their places in the courtroom for the action a few days earlier when the trial began.* IGGIE THE PIGGIE *is on the stand.*

Judge: Please state your full name for the jury.

Iggie: Iggie the Piggie.

Judge: Your witness, Mr. Wolf.

Wolf: Iggie, how long have you known the defendant?

Iggie: Who's the defendant?

Wolf: Me! The wolf!

Iggie: Oh. Two weeks, I guess.

Wolf: You guess? Do you always guess when you answer questions in a court of law?

Iggie: I don't know.

Wolf: You don't know?

Iggie: I've never been in a court of law before.

Wolf: Me neither; aren't you nervous?

Iggie: Yes, I am. *(pointing to the JURY)* Who are they?

Wolf: They're the jury. They decide if I did it or not.

Judge *(getting impatient):* Can we get on with it?

Wolf: I'm sorry, your Honor. *(to IGGIE)* Please tell the court about the first day we met.

Iggie: My two brothers were over at my brick house.

Wolf: For the record, your Honor, Iggie the Piggie refers to his brothers, Squiggy and Moe.

Judge *(surprised at the corny names):* Iggie, Squiggy, and Moe?

Iggie: Well, your Honor, my parents already had an Iggie and a Squiggy, and they thought they should have one Moe.

★ *Blackout*

Scene 2

★ *Inside* IGGIE's *brick house.* IGGIE, SQUIGGY, *and* MOE *are huddling in the corner, trembling with fright.* WOLF *is at the side of the stage, looking mean.*

Wolf *(in a mean voice):* Little pigs! Little pigs! Let me come in!

Iggie: Not by the hair of my chinney chin chin!

Squiggy: You tell 'im, Iggie!

Iggie: Thanks, Squiggy!

Wolf: Then I'll huff and I'll puff and I'll blow your house into another galaxy! *(He tries huffing and puffing and cannot blow down the brick house.)* Let me in, little pigs, or I'll make you my supper!

Moe: What did he say?

Squiggy: He says he'll make us his supper!

Iggie: He'll make us his supper? Don't worry, brothers. My brick house is strong enough to protect us from the evil wolf!

★ WOLF *tries to blow down the house and he cannot. The piggies dance in celebration.*

★ *Lights fade.*

Scene 3

★ *Back in the courtroom, at the trial*

Judge: Thank you, Iggie the Piggie. Do you have anything else to ask, Mr. Wolf?

Wolf: Yes, your Honor, I would like to call Squiggy and Moe to the stand.

Judge: Squiggy and Moe, please take the stand.

★ *SQUIGGY and MOE take the stand with IGGIE. All three sit in the same chair.*

Wolf: What do you think I said outside your brick house? On the day in question?

Iggie: I thought you said, "I'll huff and I'll puff and blow you into another galaxy!"

Squiggy: I thought he said, "My hands are rough. Can I borrow some moisturizing lotion?"

Moe: I thought he said, "I'll have a BLT on whole wheat—hold the mayo!"

Wolf: So you admit that you really aren't sure what I said. (*to JURY*) I intend to prove that sometimes we don't hear everything clearly. Some people don't pay attention. . . .

Judge *(trying to get WOLF's attention)*: Mr. Wolf . . .

Wolf *(continuing without hearing the judge)*: Some people only hear what they want to hear . . .

Judge *(again trying to interrupt WOLF)*: Mr. Wolf . . .

Wolf *(again he does not hear)*: And some people have wax . . .

Judge *(finally interrupting)*: Mr. Wolf, please make your point.

Wolf: Judge, with your permission, I would like to explain what really happened that day I met the three pigs.

Judge: All right, Mr. Wolf. But make it snappy!

★ *Blackout*

Scene 4

★ *Back at the brick house. The pigs are sitting around playing Monopoly.*

Moe *(moving his game piece around the board)*: 1 . . . 2 . . . 3 . . . Go directly to jail? Darn!

Iggie *(taking the dice from MOE)*: My turn!

★ *They continue playing as WOLF enters the stage outside of their house.*

Wolf *(talking to himself)*: I always get a flat tire out in the middle of nowhere! Now all I've got to do is find a phone! *(He notices the brick house.)* Maybe the people who live in this brick house will let me call the motor club from their phone!

★ *WOLF begins to knock on the door of the pigs' house.*

Wolf: Hello, hello!

Iggie *(to his brothers)*: Who's that?

Squiggy: Well, it can't be the Chinese food. That already came.

Moe: Maybe it's the three bears, Harry, Mary, and Epstein.

Squiggy: Those are the three little kittens. The three bears are named Fritzie, Mitzie, and Hasenfrasen.

Iggie: No, no. They're the three blind mice! The three bears are named Enrico, Pico, and Kinnicinnic.

★ *The three of them begin to argue, all talking at once. WOLF knocks again to stop their arguing.*

Moe: I'll look out the window and SEE who it is. *(He looks.)* Hey, it's the big bad wolf!

Iggie *(clinging to his brother)*: A big bad wolf—I'm scared!

Squiggy: Just relax, brothers—he cannot hurt us in this strong brick house.

Wolf *(still talking to himself)*: What does this welcome mat say? "The house of the three little pigs." *(knocking and calling through the door)* Little pigs . . . little pigs! Let me in! I've got a flat on the interstate, and I need to call a tow truck!

Iggie: Not by the hair of my chinney chin chin!

Squiggy: You tell 'im, Iggie!

Iggie: Thanks, Squiggy!

Wolf: Please! I'm so out of breath from walking all

the way from my car. I'm huffing and puffing, and I need to blow my nose.

★ *They don't let him in.*

Squiggy: What did he say?

Wolf: Please help me, little pigs. I'm so hungry—I haven't had any supper!

Moe: What did he say?

Squiggy: He says he'll make us his supper!

Iggie: He'll make us his supper? Don't worry, brothers. My brick house is strong enough to protect us from the evil wolf!

Wolf *(still knocking)*: Please help!

★ *Lights fade.*

Scene 5

★ *The courtroom*

Judge: Members of the jury, please understand that the Piggies have appeared as character witnesses. It is your job to decide who was telling the truth. We will now hear from two more character witnesses. *(to OFFICER ONE)* Officer One? Please call Hansel and Gretel to the stand.

Officer One *(turning to OFFICER TWO)*: Officer Two? Please call Hansel and Gretel to the stand.

Officer Two *(turning to OFFICER THREE)*: Officer Three? Please call Hansel and Gretel to the stand.

Officer Three: Officer Ffff . . . *(seeing that there is nobody else to delegate)* Hansel and Gretel, please take the stand!

★ *HANSEL and GRETEL take the stand.*

Wolf: Your Honor, I plan to reveal to the court that I could not possibly have eaten Old Red because I was saving the lives of these two children. *(to the children)* Please state your names for the court.

Hansel: Hansel.

Gretel: Gretel.

Wolf: Where did we first meet?

Gretel: At Witchie Pot Pie's house.

Wolf: And how did you happen to arrive there?

Hansel: My sister and I lost our way in the woods . . .

Gretel: It wasn't my fault. I told him to leave a trail.

Hansel: I keep telling you. I did leave a trail!

Gretel: You don't leave a trail of bread crumbs in a forest full of hungry little animals!

★ *Blackout*

★ *Lights shift to the* HANSEL *and* GRETEL *setting.*

Scene 6

★ *Flashback to the woods outside* WITCHIE POT PIE'S *candy house.* WOODSMAN *and* WOODSWOMAN *enter with a lantern looking for their children.*

Woodsman: Hansel! Gretel!

Woodswoman: Gretel! Hansel!

Woodsman: Children! Where are you?

Woodswoman: They're nowhere to be found! What shall we do? Oh, it's my fault! If only I hadn't been so greedy about the firewood! I never should have sent them alone into the forest. What shall become of them?

Woodsman: Now, now. We shall find them. I know every inch of these woods. I will not give up until I've found our dear children. Their legs are short. They could not have gone far . . . unless . . .

Woodswoman: Unless what?

Woodsman: There are demons, witches, and evil spirits who inhabit these woods. They come out at night.

Woodswoman *(frightened)*: Oh, my poor children. What shall become of them?

Woodsman: Do not fret! We will find them!

★ *They exit.*

★ *CHICKEN LITTLE enters in a fright.*

Chicken Little: *It's falling! It's falling!*
Tomorrow you'll be crawling
Under piles of clouds and sky.
It's frightful! Appalling!
There isn't any stalling.
How I wish these wings could fly!

I'd fly away above the sky
On Venus I would live.
The moon would be my neighbor
And there'd be no one to give the word . . .

It's falling! It's falling!
I tell ya that I'm bawling.

This news of doom I will be spreading
near and far.
I am getting very tired. How I wish I had a car!
It's falling! It's falling!
Tomorrow you'll be crawling
Under piles of clouds and sky.

★ *CHICKEN LITTLE exits.*

★ *HANSEL and GRETEL enter, looking lost.*

Gretel: Where are we, Brother? I thought we left a trail!

Hansel: We did leave one, Sister. Only I fear that I had no stones to drop behind us to mark our way.

Gretel: What did you drop, Brother?

Hansel: Bread crumbs from my peanut butter and pickle sandwich.

Gretel *(very angry)*: BREAD CRUMBS! The birds and animals of the forest must have eaten them all up!

Hansel: What are we to do?

Gretel: We must try to find our way on our own.

★ *They come upon a house made of gingerbread and candy.*

Hansel: Look at that candy house.

Gretel: It looks good enough to eat!

Hansel: It is making me very hungry.

Gretel: Let's take a small bite . . . no one will know!

Witchie Pot Pie *(from inside the house)*: Who is nibbling on my house?

Hansel: What was that?

Witchie Pot Pie *(entering)*: Who is nibbling? Nibbling, nibbling on my house?

Gretel: I am sorry, old woman. We are lost and haven't eaten a thing all day.

Hansel: We are very hungry. May we eat your door post?

★ *CHICKEN LITTLE enters with TURKEY LURKEY and HENNY PENNY. HANSEL, GRETEL, and WITCHIE POT PIE look at the three birds as if they have wandered into the wrong story.*

All Three Birds: *It's falling! It's falling!*
Tomorrow you'll be crawling
Under piles of clouds and sky.

Henny Penny: *It's frightful! Appalling! There isn't*
any stalling.

Turkey Lurkey: *How I wish these wings could*
fly! (flap, flap)
I'd fly away above the sky
On Venus I would live.

Chicken Little: *The moon would be my neighbor*
And there'd be no one to give the word . . .

All Three Birds: *It's falling! It's falling!*

I tell ya that I'm bawling.
This news of doom I will be
spreading near and far.
I am getting very tired. How I wish I had a car!
It's falling! It's falling!
Tomorrow you'll be crawling
Under piles of clouds and sky.

★ *The three of them exit.*

Witchie Pot Pie: Come inside and I'll give you some
sweets, children.

★ *Blackout*

Scene 7

★ *The courtroom.* HANSEL *and* GRETEL *are finishing their story.*

Hansel: Then she put us in a cage until the wolf came by and rescued us.

Woodsman *(standing in his place on stage, crying tears of joy)*: Thank you, Mr. Wolf, for saving my children!

Judge: Order in the court! Mr. Wolf, do you have any further questions for these witnesses?

Wolf: Just a few, your Honor. Hansel, Gretel—how would you describe me?

Gretel: Well . . . you're about 4 foot 9 and furry. . . .

Wolf: No, I mean as a person. . . .

Hansel: You were very kind to us!

Wolf: I rest my case!

★ HANSEL *and* GRETEL *leave the witness stand.*

Judge: Officer One, please call Little Red Riding Hood to the stand.

Officer One *(turning to* OFFICER TWO*)*: Officer Two,

please call Little Red to the stand.

Officer Two *(turning to* OFFICER THREE*)*: Officer Three, please call Little Red to the stand.

Officer Three: Officer Ffff . . . *(turning to see there is not another officer)* . . . um . . . Little Red Riding Hood, please take the stand.

★ *LITTLE RED skips up to the witness stand and sits down.*

Little Red: The wolf ate my grandma! He came to her door and ate her up! I always visit on Thursdays! Last Thursday she was gone! He must have eaten her up. I say X-ray his stomach and look for her bifocals!

Wolf: I never even met your grandmother. I am going to explain what really happened that day.

★ *End of Scene*

Scene 8

★ BIG RED, *LITTLE RED's mother, is sending her off to bring a basket of goodies to* LITTLE RED's *grandmother,* OLD RED.

Big Red: Now remember, Daughter, go to Grandma's with this basket of goodies and do not stray from the path. Do not talk to strangers. Do not pick the flowers. Do not speak out of turn. Do not pass go. Do not run in the halls. Do not chew gum in school. And don't count your chickens!

★ CHICKEN LITTLE *enters with* TURKEY LURKEY *and* HENNY PENNY.

Chicken Little: Did somebody mention chickens?

Turkey Lurkey: Or turkeys?

Henny Penny: Or hennys?

All Three Birds: *It's falling! It's falling!*
Tomorrow you'll be crawling
Under piles of clouds and sky.

Henny: *It's frightful! Appalling!*
There isn't any stalling . . .

Turkey: *How I wish these wings could fly!*
I'd fly away above the sky
On Venus I would live . . .

Chicken: *The moon would be my neighbor*
And there'd be no one to give the word . . .

All Three Birds: *It's falling! It's falling!*
I tell ya that I'm bawling.
This news of doom I will be
spreading near and far.
I am getting very tired. How I wish I had a car!
It's falling! It's falling!
Tomorrow you'll be crawling
Under piles of clouds and sky.

★ *The three of them exit.*

★ *LITTLE RED walks around the stage, then stops at*
OLD RED's house. She knocks on the door. WITCHIE
POT PIE is inside, disguised as a wolf.

Witchie Pot Pie *(evilly)*: With this disguise Little
Red will think that I am the wolf and I ate her
grandmother. This way I can get back at that nasty
wolf who helped those delicious little children,
Hansel and Gretel, escape! And I can also get back at
Little Red Riding Hood's grandmother, my sweet
twin sister! Yuck!

★ *WITCHIE POT PIE opens the door. LITTLE RED thinks*
that she is talking to her grandma.

Little Red: Here is a basket of goodies for the best
grandma in the world!

Witchie Pot Pie: I am not your grandma! I am

the big bad wolf!

Little Red *(not paying attention)*: Grandma! What big eyes you have!

Witchie Pot Pie: These are wolf eyes! Why don't you open yours and take a look?

Little Red: Grandma! What big ears you have!

Witchie Pot Pie: I'm not your granny! Open up your ears so I can tell you I'm the big bad wolf!

Little Red *(not paying attention)*: Grandma! What big wolflike teeth you have!

Witchie Pot Pie: You better believe it, baby! What do you have to say about that?

Little Red: So how've you been, Grandma?

★ *WITCHIE POT PIE roars with anger.*

Little Red: Sore throat still?

★ *WITCHIE POT PIE roars again.*

Little Red: Eek!

★ *A big chase follows that involves many cast members. We end up in the courtroom with the JURY about to announce the verdict.*

Scene 9

★ *The courtroom. The* JUDGE *and* JURY *are seated.* WOLF *is downstage center.*

Wolf *(to audience)*: See? I couldn't have eaten Old Red! All the evidence is in. All of the witnesses have testified. I guess I have to find out what the jury decides sooner or later. *(to audience)* Have you made up your mind? You don't think I did it, do you? *(pointing to the* JURY*)* Let's see what they think.

★ *The* JUDGE *and the* JURY *unfreeze and the* JURY *is about to give its verdict.*

Judge: Jury, have you reached a verdict?

Tom: Yes—

Sue: your . . .

Ted: Honor.

Ann: We . . .

Pat: find . . .

Sam: the . . .

Tom: wolf . . .

Sue: guilty

Ted: as

Ann: charged.

Pat: Guilty.

Sam: Guilty.

Tom: Guilty.

Sue: Guilty.

Ted: Guilty.

Ann: Guilty

Pat: as

Sam: charged!

★ *Suddenly from stage left OLD RED enters.*

Old Red *(singing to herself)***:** Oh, I wanna go back to my little grass shack in Ka Wala Ka Koo Hawaii! La La La La La La La La La La.

★ *LITTLE RED is surprised.*

Little Red: Grandma!

Witchie Pot Pie *(seeing that she will soon be found out)*: Uh-oh!

Wolf: See! I told you I didn't eat her!

Old Red: I'm back! *(to WITCHIE POT PIE)* Thank you, dear sister, for sending me on that lovely vacation. You know, I don't think I'll ever be able to get over how surprised I was when you offered me the trip. I always thought you didn't like me. I know better now, sweet sister!

Witchie Pot Pie: Don't sweet sister me. . . . You always come in at the wrong time!

Judge: Jury—I think that we all owe Mr. Wolf an apology. We can only hope that he will accept it.

Wolf: Oh, I accept. It is not easy to see both sides of a story. But you'll never see the other side if you don't look!

Witchie Pot Pie: This is all so sweet and mushy, I think I'm going to be sick! You all celebrate—I'm going home.

Little Red: Wait! Stay and celebrate with us! Grandma is going to teach us all to hula!

★ *WITCHIE POT PIE stays on stage, looking defeated.*

Wolf: What's a hula?

Little Red: It's a dance!

Old Red: I picked it up in Hawaii. You're going to love it!

★ *Suddenly a loud boom is heard and clouds fall to the stage.*

All Three Birds (*entering*):
>*It's falling! It's falling!*
>*We told you it was falling!*
>*But you did not hear, did you?*
>*We told you—We warned you.*
>*We did not want to scorn you.*
>*But, the foot's on the other shoe.*
>
>*It is always good to listen to*
>*Another point of view.*
>*Hear all sides of the story and*
>*You'll have a better clue.*
>
>*We're happy, there's justice.*
>*You'll really have to trust us.*
>*We want you all to go out yelling up to every rafter,*
>*The wolves and pigs, the reds and grets,*
>*Live happily ever after!*

★ *Curtain*